*This book was a gift
to our library
from Capstone Press.*

D1267325

First Facts™

Holidays and Culture

Juneteenth

Jubilee for Freedom

by June Preszler

Consultant:
Sandra Adell, Professor of Literature
Department of Afro-American Studies
University of Wisconsin, Madison

Capstone
press®
Mankato, Minnesota

First Facts is published by Capstone Press,
151 Good Counsel Drive, P.O. Box 669, Mankato, Minnesota 56002.
www.capstonepress.com

Library of Congress Cataloging-in-Publication Data
Preszler, June, 1954-
    Juneteenth : jubilee for freedom / by June Preszler.
    p. cm.—(First facts. Holidays and culture)
    Summary: "Describes the history and meaning of Juneteenth and how it is celebrated
today"—Provided by publisher.
    Includes bibliographical references and index.
    ISBN-13: 978-0-7368-6396-4 (hardcover)
    ISBN-10: 0-7368-6396-6 (hardcover)
    1. Juneteenth—Juvenile literature. 2. African Americans—Texas—Galveston—Social life and
customs—Juvenile literature. 3. Slaves—Emancipation—United States—Juvenile literature.
4. African Americans—Anniversaries, etc.—Juvenile literature. 5. African Americans—Social life
and customs—Juvenile literature. 6. Galveston (Tex.)—Social life and customs—Juvenile
literature. I. Title. II. Series.
E185.93.T4P74 2007
94.263—dc22
                                                                              2006002948

Editorial Credits
Shari Joffe, editor; Biner Design, designer; Juliette Peters, set designer; Jo Miller, photo researcher;
    Scott Thoms, photo editor

Photo Credits
AP/Wide World Photos/Thomas Terry, 20
Austin History Center, Austin Public Library/PICA 05481, 11
Capstone Press/Karon Dubke, 21
Corbis/Ariel Skelley, 13
Donna Lamb, cover
Getty Images Inc./David Paul Morris, 1, 18
The Image Works/Bob Daemmrich, 7, 14; Jeff Greenberg, 16–17
Library of Congress, 8
PhotoEdit Inc./Bob Daemmrich, 15; Tom Carter, 4–5,19

1 2 3 4 5 6 11 10 09 08 07 06

Table of Contents

Celebrating Juneteenth

Soulful blues music fills the air. Children laugh and play baseball or tug-of-war. When the music stops, a speaker begins. He talks about a time when African Americans were slaves. He tells the story of Juneteenth. Listeners learn how slaves in Texas first heard they were free.

What Is Juneteenth?

Each year on June 19, millions of people celebrate the end of slavery after the Civil War (1861–1865). Juneteenth honors the **sacrifices** and successes of African Americans. It is a day when African Americans take pride in their **heritage**.

Fact!

People combined "June" and "nineteenth" to create the name Juneteenth.

General Gordon Granger

The Last to Know

Slaves in Galveston, Texas, were the last U.S. slaves to hear about their freedom. The news came more than two years after President Abraham Lincoln ended slavery in some southern states in 1863. Union troops led by General Gordon Granger brought the news of freedom on June 19, 1865.

Fact!

Why did it take so long for Texas slaves to learn they were free? Union troops didn't reach Texas during the Civil War. There was no one to force Texas slave owners to free their slaves until the war ended in 1865.

A New Holiday

June 19 became a day of celebration for African Americans in Texas. People prayed and elders told stories of the past. Over time, barbecuing, fishing, music, and games became part of the festivities. People gave speeches about **self-improvement**. The **traditions** soon spread to other states.

Fact!

At some early Juneteenth events, people threw old, ragged clothing into rivers to show they were no longer slaves.

11

Juneteenth at Home

Today, many families decorate their homes with red banners on Juneteenth. Red stands for the blood that people shed as slaves.

The holiday brings families together. They tell stories of their history. They make plans to help end **racism** in the world.

Juneteenth Around Town

Juneteenth means exciting activities.
Adults and children march in parades.
Axes are sometimes carried because they
were used to cut the chains of slavery.

Crowds gather at picnics. Fishing contests, baseball games, and sack races have been part of Juneteenth events for many years.

Food

Juneteenth celebrations include lots of good food. Barbecuing is as important today as it was during early Juneteenth events. People simmer pork or lamb in the barbecue pit, just as newly freed slaves did. They enjoy **symbolic** red foods like strawberry soda and red velvet cake.

Music

Many Juneteenth celebrations
include music with African American
roots. The exciting sounds of jazz,
blues, and hip-hop fill the air.

18

Through music, food, and fun,
people celebrate the end of slavery. On
Juneteenth, African Americans honor the
past and look toward a bright future.

Amazing Holiday Story!

Texas was the last place to get the news that slavery was over. But it was the first state to make Juneteenth an official state holiday. In 1980, Texas State Representative Al Edwards helped Juneteenth become a Texas state holiday. Juneteenth became the first official African American holiday in the United States.

Hands On: Paper Chain

Red is the traditional color of Juneteenth. Make a red paper chain to hang in your home or yard to celebrate Juneteenth.

What You Need
1 piece of red construction paper
scissors
ruler
pencil
crayons or markers
glue stick

What You Do
1. On the piece of paper, use a ruler to mark off 1-inch- (2.5-centimeter-) wide strips. Cut out the strips.
2. With a crayon or marker, print words on the strips that are important to remember on Juneteenth. Words might include "freedom," "hopes," and "goals."
3. Form one of the strips into a circle and glue the ends together.
4. Form the next circle and loop it into the first circle. Glue the ends. Repeat until you've used all of your strips. You can make your chain as long as you want by using more pieces of paper.
5. Share the words on your chain, and tell friends why they are important ideas to remember.

Glossary

heritage (HER-uh-tij)—history and traditions handed down from the past

racism (RAY-si-zim)—thinking that a particular race is better than others

sacrifice (SAK-ruh-fise)—to give up something important or enjoyable for a good reason

self-improvement (SELF-im-PROOV-muhnt)—the process of becoming a better, more educated person

symbolic (sim-BAHL-ic)—standing for something else

tradition (truh-DISH-uhn)—a custom, idea, or belief that is passed down through time

Read More

Jordan, Denise M. *Juneteenth Day.* Holiday Histories. Chicago: Heinemann Library, 2003.

Leeper, Angela. *Juneteenth: A Day to Celebrate Freedom from Slavery.* Berkeley Heights, N.J.: Enslow, 2004.

Rosinsky, Natalie M. *Juneteenth.* Let's See. Minneapolis: Compass Point Books, 2004.

Internet Sites

FactHound offers a safe, fun way to find Internet sites related to this book. All of the sites on FactHound have been researched by our staff.

Here's how:

1. Visit *www.facthound.com*

2. Choose your grade level.

3. Type in this book ID **0736863966** for age-appropriate sites. You may also browse subjects by clicking on letters, or by clicking on pictures and words.

4. Click on the **Fetch It** button.

FactHound will fetch the best sites for you!

Index